CONTENTS

his picture was taken on KODAK EKTACHROME Infrared Film using a No. 11 green filter and a transmission diffraction grating. For more information on diffraction gratings, see page 57.

picture on page 4.

A polarizing screen combined with deliberate underexposure produced this nearly black sky effect. See pages 22-26 for information on using polarizing screens.

HOW FILTERS WORK

Both black-and-white and color pictures are usually made with colored light reflected from a subject. Most pictures are made of colored objects because both black and white are the exceptions in nature; colors are the rule. Understanding the nature of color and colored light will help you select a film/filter combination to achieve the result you want in your pictures.

White light is the sum of all the colors of the rainbow, while black is the absence of all the colors. For practical purposes, we can consider white light as composed of the three primary light colors—red, green, and blue. When one or two of these colors are subtracted or absorbed, we see the color that is left. For example, if green and blue are subtracted, we see red. Colors in nature are usually not pure, because absorption and reflection are rarely complete. Most of the time, we see a mixture of colors with one color predominating. All natural colors are made up of the primary colors—red, green, and blue.

Each of us sees colors in a very personal way. Our perception of a color is influenced by the surrounding colors and brightness level, the surface gloss of an object, and the degree and type of our color blindness. Different types of films also see colors in different ways. Black-and-white films may record a color as a lighter or darker shade of gray than we expect. By using filters with black-and-white films, you can control the shades of gray to obtain a technically correct rendition of your subject or to exaggerate or suppress the tonal differences for visibility, emphasis, or other effects. By using filters with color films, you can change the color quality of the light source to get the proper color rendition or to create special effects.

TYPES AND SIZES

Filters are available in three forms: optical glass disks bound with metal rims, lacquered gelatin-film squares, and glass squares. The glass-disk filters are the most practical for general use. They're available in different sizes called series numbers, such as Series 4, 5, and 6, to fit almost any camera. Or they may be specified by their diameter in millimeters.

You attach glass-disk filters to a camera in one of two ways. Some filters are threaded so that you can screw them directly into the lens mount. But on most cameras, you need a device called an adapter ring to hold the filter over the lens.

Adapter rings either screw into the lens mount or slip on over it. Check your camera manual for the type and size of adapter ring you need. Sizes of adapter rings are expressed in terms of the filter series number that the ring accepts and a measurement in millimeters. This measurement is the diameter of the lens mount (not the focal length of the lens). For example, a lens with a 50 mm focal length might require a Series 5, 28.5 mm adapter ring. This ring would accept any Series 5 filter. A retaining ring holds the filter in the adapter ring. If you want to use two glass-disk filters at the same time or a filter and a close-up lens, you can use a lens hood or a second retaining ring to hold the second filter in place.

Your photo dealer can help you select glass-disk filters of the appropriate size for your camera. Eastman Kodak Company does not manufacture glass-disk filters, but they are distributed by other companies, including these:

Hal's Fotographics,
P.O. Box 80726,
Chamblee, Ga. 30341

Harrison & Harrison,
6363 Santa Monica Blvd.,
Hollywood, Calif. 90038

Ponder & Best, Inc.,
1630 Stewart St.,
Santa Monica, Calif. 90406

P. R. O.,
159 W. 33rd St.,
New York, N.Y. 10001

Samigon Div./Argraph Corp.,
Carlstadt, N.J. 07072

Soligor, c/o AIC Photo Inc.,
168 Glen Cove Road,
Carle Place, N.Y. 15514

Spiratone, Inc.,
135-06 Northern Blvd.,
Flushing, N.Y. 11354

Tiffen Manufacturing Corp.,
71 Jane St.,
Roslyn Hts., N.Y. 11577

Uniphot, Inc.,
61-10 34th Ave.,
Woodside, N.Y. 11377

Gelatin-film squares are the least expensive type of filter. They scratch easily, so handle them carefully by the edges. You can hold them in front of the lens, but it may be more convenient to attach them to your camera with a KODAK Gelatin Filter Frame Holder and a KODAK Gelatin Filter Frame.

Glass-square filters are a more durable version of the gelatin filters. They consist of gelatin squares bound between two squares of glass for protection. You can hold glass-square filters in front of the lens, or attach them to the camera with a KODAK Gelatin Filter Frame Holder. With glass-square filters, you don't need to use a Gelatin Filter Frame.

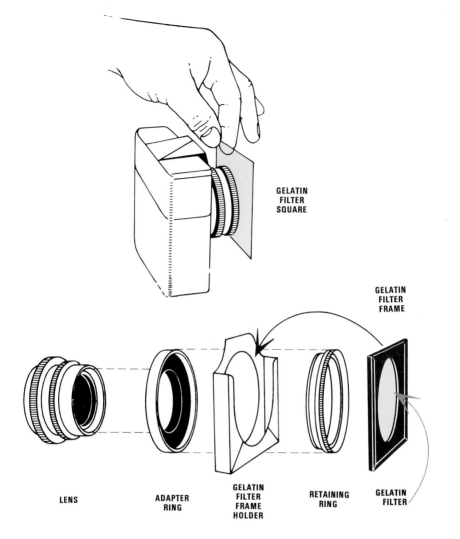

GELATIN
FILTER
SQUARE

GELATIN
FILTER
FRAME

| LENS | ADAPTER RING | GELATIN FILTER FRAME HOLDER | RETAINING RING | GELATIN FILTER |

FILTER DESIGNATIONS

Filter designations such as K2, A, G, etc, were assigned many years ago, when the number of filters required for photographic work was quite small and when a simple identification system was adequate. As the need for additional filters became apparent, the present numbering system was adopted, replacing the old alphanumeric designations. Because published literature frequently contains references to the older designations only, both current and discontinued designations are shown here.

Current Designations	Discontinued Designations
No. 6	K1
No. 8	K2
No. 9	K3
No. 11	X1
No. 13	X2
No. 15	G
No. 25	A
No. 29	F
No. 47	C5
No. 49	C4
No. 58	B
No. 61	N

LIGHT AND COLOR

You don't need to know everything about how filters work to use them effectively. The filter tables in this book, the *KODAK Master Photoguide* (AR-21), or the *KODAK Professional Photoguide* (R-28), sold by photo dealers, will help you select the proper filter for most subjects. However, you may be curious about why filters produce the effects they do in your pictures. Also, understanding how filters work may help you decide whether you need to use a filter for a certain picture and which filter will produce the effect you want. To understand how filters work, you need some basic information on light and color.

Red

First let's consider why we call a filter "red." White light, consisting of a mixture of blue, green, and red, falls upon the filter, but the filter appears red because it lets through only the red light. It absorbs (subtracts) the blue and green light.

Similarly, a piece of red paper is red because it reflects red light. The white light falling on it consists of a mixture of blue, green, and red. The red paper absorbs the blue and green light, but reflects the red light. Therefore, anything that absorbs (subtracts) both blue and green light will look red.

Color as seen in white light	Colors of light absorbed
Red	Blue and green
Blue	Red and green
Green	Red and blue
Yellow (red plus green)	Blue
Magenta (red-blue)	Green
Cyan (blue-green)	Red
Black	Red, green, and blue
White	None
Gray	Equal portions of red, green, and blue

This is the key to an understanding of photographic filters: They always subtract some of the light reflected from a scene before the light reaches the film in your camera. You should understand this aspect of color to get the best results in your black-and-white pictures of colored objects. (Remember that in the negative/positive process, areas that are light on the negative will be dark in the print. When a filter absorbs a certain color of light so that objects of that color have less density on the negative, those objects will be darker in the print.) Get into the habit of thinking of a red filter not so much as one that's red, but as one

REFLECTION

Object absorbs green and blue, looks red.

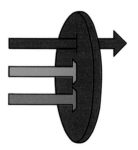

TRANSMISSION

Filter absorbs green and blue, looks red.

that absorbs blue and green. This concept is important because it defines the filter in terms of how it affects the light reflected from your subject to the film.

Yellow

A yellow filter is one that absorbs blue light. Likewise, a yellow sunflower absorbs blue light and reflects the other parts of white light—red and green. Our eyes see a mixture of red and green as *yellow* (lack of blue).

You may know that placing a yellow filter over the camera lens greatly improves black-and-white pictures of landscapes containing blue skies and white clouds. In a picture made without a filter, the blue sky may be rendered as a very light gray or white, too close to the tonal value of the clouds to provide separation between the two. A yellow filter absorbs the blue light, making the blue sky appear darker in the print. The clouds, which reflect light of all colors, are not darkened and they stand out in contrast.

Green

Since white light consists of a mixture of red, green, and blue, it is obvious that green is white light minus both red and blue. The green we see in nature, such as foliage green, is impure because foliage reflects quite a lot of blue and red. Foliage looks slightly darker than we expect when it is photographed on black-and-white film without a filter. By using a yellow or yellow-green filter to absorb some of the unwanted blue and red light, you can record foliage in its proper gray tone.

This may seem to imply a contradiction: that it is the filter which gives foliage a lighter gray value. If a filter subtracts light, there will be less density on the negative and the print will be darker, so how does the filter make foliage lighter? Actually, the filter darkens the rendering of the colors it absorbs, thus making the colors it transmits lighter by comparison. This becomes apparent when the negative is correctly printed.

Let's assume that we have a simple scene made up of blue sky, white clouds, and green foliage. The proportions of red, blue, and green in the light from these surfaces vary, as shown in the diagram (page 10). Therefore, a yellow filter subtracts the greatest proportion of light from the sky, and the smallest proportion from the foliage. The individual brightnesses have one relationship in the scene, but the filter alters the relative brightnesses that reach the film. To clarify this numerically, let's say that the scene brightnesses have this rela-

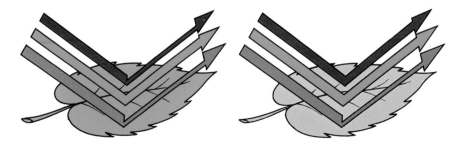

Foliage green reflects green, most of the blue, and a little of the red. The yellow of flowers and foliage reflects red, green, and a little of the blue.

tionship: cloud, 20; sky, 16; foliage, 8. The filter changes this relationship to cloud, 14; sky, 8; foliage, 7. (These are not real values—just arbitrary ones.) In a correctly exposed negative, you will see that the filter has increased the density difference between cloud and sky and decreased the density difference between sky and foliage. When the negative is correctly printed, the sky tone will be darker, the clouds will show up, and

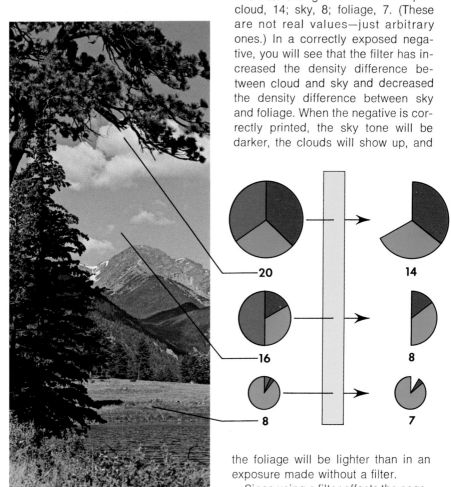

A yellow filter absorbs the blue component of the light reflected from all parts of the scene. The light affecting the film thus has a greater brightness contrast between white cloud and blue sky and a decreased brightness contrast between green foliage and sky and cloud. Consequently, greens are lighter, and the tone separation between sky and cloud is better.

the foliage will be lighter than in an exposure made without a filter.

Since using a filter affects the negative densities, correct exposure in the camera is important for maximum effect. Overexposure may add so much to the densities that the effect of the filter will be canceled. Correct printing is also important. Selecting an incorrect grade of paper, or using an incorrect exposure time, or both can cancel the effect you wanted.

This picture was taken without a filter.

Recording this scene through a No. 15 deep-yellow filter darkened the blue sky and emphasized the white clouds.

PETER GALES

Sky Conditions

Another factor which affects the amount of control that filters will have on skies is the atmospheric condition. Filters have the greatest effect on a deep-blue sky. As haze or overcast increases, the sky becomes less blue, so the effect of filters decreases even to the point where they have no effect at all.

FILTER FACTORS

Because filters subtract some of the light passing through the lens, you need to increase either your exposure time or the lens opening to make up for this loss of light. The number by which you must multiply the exposure you would use without a filter is called the filter factor. Thus if a filter has a factor of two, you must either double your exposure time or open the lens aperture one full stop. For example, the usual exposure outdoors in sunlight for KODAK PLUS-X Pan Film is 1/125 second at $f/16$. When you use a No. 8 yellow filter, which has a filter factor of 2 with that film, you must either change the shutter speed to 1/60 second or open the lens aperture to $f/11$.

11

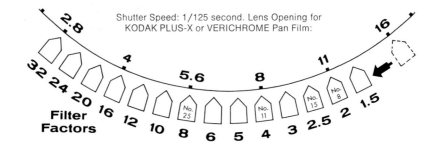

Shutter Speed: 1/125 second. Lens Opening for KODAK PLUS-X or VERICHROME Pan Film:

The diagram above shows the relationship between *f*-numbers and filter factors. Since it applies directly to photographing sunlit subjects on KODAK PLUS-X Pan or KODAK VERICHROME Pan Film at 1/125 second, the correct lens opening without a filter is *f*/16. The lens openings and filter factors for four of the most popular filters are also shown. To adapt this diagram to a panchromatic film with a different film speed, use a shutter speed that still requires *f*/16 for an unfiltered exposure in sunlight.

If you use a filter and a polarizing screen together, the filter factor is the product of their individual factors. For example, if you use a polarizing screen (factor of 2.5) plus a filter with a factor of 2, your total filter factor will be 5. So you should multiply your exposure time by 5 or increase the lens opening by 2⅓ stops.

Published filter factors apply to average conditions. You may have to make some modifications. If your results aren't satisfactory when you use the published factors, establish your own factors by making exposure tests.

In practice, you can take some liberty in applying filter factors, particularly in using yellow filters for sky control. For example, if you make no compensation for the filter and intentionally cause a slight underexposure, you may increase the contrast in the sky rendering.

For all practical purposes, if your camera has a through-the-lens metering system you don't have to consider the filter factor. Since the meter is reading the light through the filter, the meter will indicate which lens opening or shutter speed you should use. Check your camera manual for details on how to use filters with your particular metering system.

Factors Depend on Light and Film

The filter-factor value depends on the light source and film type, in addition to the absorption of the filter.

A No. 15 deep yellow filter has a daylight factor of 2.5 with KODAK PLUS-X Pan Film and similar films. However, when you use tungsten light with these films, the filter factor is 1.5.

The reason for the difference in factors is understandable when you consider the color quality of the light sources. Daylight contains much ultraviolet and blue light. Light from photoflood and other tungsten lamps contains less blue and much less ultraviolet. Since the No. 15 filter is deep yellow, it stops a higher proportion of usable light from daylight than from tungsten light; therefore it requires more exposure compensation when you use it in daylight.

The table on page 21 gives the filter factors for some common filters with Kodak black-and-white films.

PETER GALES

A No. 25 red filter is often used for pictorial landscape photography because it provides dramatic contrast between the clouds and the blue sky.

FILTERS FOR BLACK-AND-WHITE PICTURES

The filters used in black-and-white picture-taking can be divided into three main types: (1) *Correction filters* change the response of the film so that all colors are recorded at approximately the relative brightness values seen by the eye. (2) *Contrast filters* change the relative brightness values so that two colors that would otherwise record as nearly the same shade of gray will have decidedly different brightnesses in the picture. (3) *Haze filters* reduce the effects of aerial haze.

13

Here's the way the original scene looked.

This picture, taken without a filter, does not reproduce the scene with the same relative brightness that appeared in the original scene.

By using a No. 8 yellow filter with panchromatic film, you can reproduce the scene in the shades of gray that represent the brightness relationships your eyes saw in the original scene.

CORRECTION FILTERS

Although panchromatic films respond to all the colors the eye can see, they do not reproduce all colors with the same relative brightness that the eye sees. For example, blue and violet normally appear darker to the eye than green does, but the film is more sensitive to these colors and they look lighter than green in a black-and-white print. By using filters, you can reproduce the colors with the relative brightness that you see.

Panchromatic films are more sensitive to ultraviolet and blue light than your eyes are. To reproduce the colors in a scene in the same brightness relationship that your eye sees, you'll need to use a yellow filter to absorb the ultraviolet and some of the blue light. Use a No. 8 yellow filter with Kodak panchromatic films to reproduce a *daylight* scene in the shades of gray that represent the brightness relationship your eyes see.

Because tungsten light contains more red than daylight, you'll need to use a yellow-green filter to obtain a natural brightness relationship in scenes photographed by tungsten light. The yellow in the filter absorbs the ultraviolet and some of the blue light, while the green absorbs some of the red light. For the most natural-looking effect, use a No. 11 yellow-green filter with Kodak panchromatic films in *tungsten* light.

This picture shows the color and brightness relationships of a scene photographed under tungsten lighting.

The brightness relationships of the scene are not reproduced as the eye sees them when the scene is photographed on black-and-white film without a filter.

NEIL MONTANUS

To get the natural brightness relationships in scenes photographed by tungsten light, use a No. 11 yellow-green filter.

Red geraniums, photographed on
KODACHROME 64 Film (Daylight), look
dramatic against a background of green grass.

When the geraniums are photographed in
black-and-white without a filter, the red
and green are recorded as nearly the same
tone of gray.

A No. 25 red filter transmits the red of the
geraniums and absorbs the green of the grass.
When you use this filter, the red subjects will
appear light in a black-and-white print and
green subjects will appear dark.

A No. 58 green filter absorbs the red of the
geraniums and transmits the green of the
grass, producing dark flowers and light grass
in the black-and-white print.

CONTRAST FILTERS

Sometimes you may not want to reproduce the scene exactly as your eyes see it. You may want to increase contrast between two objects that would normally photograph as nearly the same shade of gray. You can use contrast filters to lighten or darken certain colors in the subject. For example, red geraniums and green grass may photograph as nearly the same tone of gray. If you use a No. 25 red filter, which transmits the red of the geraniums and absorbs the green of the grass, the geraniums will be light and the grass dark in your print. Since you probably think of the flowers as being brighter than the grass, this print may look natural to you. But if you use a No. 58 green filter, which absorbs the red of the geraniums and transmits the green of the grass, you'll get the opposite result: dark flowers and light grass.

You can produce unusual effects in your black-and-white pictures when you understand how filters influence brightness relationships. Remember that a filter transmits its own color, making that color lighter in a black-and-white print. To make a color darker, use a filter that will absorb that color. The table on page 20 will help you decide which filter you'll need to produce the effect you want.

Darkening Blue Skies

One of the most frequent uses of filters in black-and-white photography is to darken a blue sky so that white clouds will stand out more prominently. Use a No. 8 yellow filter to reproduce the sky as your eyes see it. You can darken the sky with a No. 15, deep-yellow filter; or for really dramatic sky effects, use a No. 25 red or No. 29 deep-red filter.

The original scene recorded on
KODACOLOR II Film.

No filter.

No. 8 yellow filter.

No. 15 deep-yellow filter.

No. 25 red filter.

No. 29 deep-red filter.

PETER GALES

17

This picture was taken without a polarizing screen.

A polarizing screen darkened the blue sky.

Using a No. 25 red filter with a polarizing screen produces dramatic skies like this one.

Polarizing Screens

A polarizing screen provides another method of darkening a blue sky. You obtain the maximum effect when you take pictures at right angles to the sun (for example, when the subject is side-lighted or the sun is overhead) and when the indicator handle on the polarizing screen (if it has one) is pointed toward the sun. For spectacular effects in black-and-white, try using a No. 8 yellow, No. 25 red, or No. 11 yellow-green filter with a polarizing screen. For more information on polarizing screens, see page 22.

Some Exceptions

The sky may appear lighter in your pictures than you would expect for these reasons:

1. A misty sky does not photograph as dark as a clear blue sky. *You can't darken an overcast sky by using a filter.*

2. The sky is frequently almost white at the horizon and shades to a more intense blue at the zenith. Therefore, the effect of the filter at the horizon is small, but it becomes greater as you aim the camera upwards.

3. The sky near the sun is less blue than the surrounding sky and therefore is less affected by a filter.

Black-and-white film is very sensitive to the ultraviolet light scattered by atmospheric haze; you may notice more haze in your pictures than you saw in the scene itself.

The No. 25 red filter absorbs ultraviolet light and reduces the effects of atmospheric haze. The filter also darkens subjects that are green, such as the tree foliage.

REDUCING THE EFFECTS OF HAZE WITH FILTERS

Distant landscapes and aerial views from high altitudes often appear to be veiled by bluish haze, even on clear days. This haze hides some of the detail when you photograph such a scene without a filter. True atmospheric haze is bluish and results from the scattering of light by very small particles of dust and water vapor and, to some extent, by the air itself. This atmospheric haze scatters a lot of ultraviolet radiation, which the eye can't see. Since the film is very sensitive to ultraviolet, you may end up with more haze in your picture than you saw when you made the photograph.

You can reduce the effects of haze in your black-and-white pictures by filtering out some of the blue light and ultraviolet radiation. The amount of recorded haze decreases with the following filters in this order: No. 8 yellow, No. 15 deep yellow, and No. 25 red.

Skylight or haze filters, which are for use with color films, do not penetrate haze. These filters are used to reduce the bluishness in pictures made in the shade and on overcast days and in those of distant scenes.

Mist and fog are white because they are composed of water droplets. Using filters will not help you to photograph a scene through mist or fog.

Filter Recommendations for
Black-and-White Films in Daylight

Subject	Effect Desired	Suggested Filter
Blue Sky	Natural	No. 8 Yellow
	Darkened	No. 15 Deep Yellow
	Spectacular	No. 25 Red
	Almost black	No. 29 Deep Red
	Night effect	No. 25 Red, plus polarizing screen
Marine Scenes When Sky Is Blue	Natural	No. 8 Yellow
	Water dark	No. 15 Deep Yellow
Sunsets	Natural	None or No. 8 Yellow
	Increased brilliance	No. 15 Deep Yellow or No. 25 Red
Distant Landscapes	Addition of haze for atmospheric effects	No. 47 Blue
	Very slight addition of haze	None
	Natural	No. 8 Yellow
	Haze reduction	No. 15 Deep Yellow
	Greater haze reduction	No. 25 Red or No. 29 Deep Red
Nearby Foliage	Natural	No. 8 Yellow or No. 11 Yellow-Green
	Light	No. 58 Green
Outdoor Portraits Against Sky	Natural	No. 11 Yellow-Green, No. 8 Yellow, or polarizing screen
Flowers—Blossoms and Foliage	Natural	No. 8 Yellow or No. 11 Yellow-Green
Red, "Bronze," Orange, and Similar Colors	Lighter to show detail	No. 25 Red
Dark Blue, Purple, and Similar Colors	Lighter to show detail	None or No. 47 Blue
Foliage Plants	Lighter to show detail	No. 58 Green
Architectural Stone, Wood, Fabrics, Sand, Snow, etc, When Sunlit and Under Blue Sky	Natural	No. 8 Yellow
	Enhanced texture rendering	No. 15 Deep Yellow or No. 25 Red

Filter Factors for KODAK Black-and-White Films*

Filter Number	Color of Filter	VERICHROME Pan, PLUS-X Pan, PANATOMIC-X, and TRI-X Pan Films			
		Daylight		Tungsten	
		Filter Factor	Open the Lens by (f-stops)	Filter Factor	Open the Lens by (f-stops)
3	Light Yellow	1.5	⅔	—	—
4	Yellow	1.5	⅔	1.5	⅔
6	Light Yellow	1.5	⅔	1.5	⅔
8	Yellow	2	1	1.5	⅔
9	Deep Yellow	2	1	1.5	⅔
11	Yellow-Green	4	2	4	2
12	Deep Yellow	2	1	1.5	⅔
13	Dark Yellow-Green	5	2⅓	4	2
15	Deep Yellow	2.5	1⅓	1.5	⅔
23A	Light Red	6	2⅔	3	1⅔
50	Deep Blue	20	4⅓	40	5⅓
25	Red	8	3	5	2⅓
58	Green	6	2⅔	6	2⅔
47	Blue	6	2⅔	12	3⅔
29	Deep Red	16	4	8	3
61	Deep Green	12	3⅔	12	3⅔
47B	Deep Blue	8	3	16	4
Polarizing Screen—Gray		2.5	1⅓	2.5	1⅓

*The filter factors for a specific film may vary somewhat from this listing. See the film instructions.

Some Lens Settings for Use with Filters

KODAK Film— Roll and 135	Average frontlighted subject in bright sunlight, shutter speed 1/125 second			
	Filter			
	No. 8	No. 11	No. 15	No. 25
PANATOMIC-X	f/5.6	f/4	f/4 ↓ 5.6	f/2.8
VERICHROME Pan	f/11	f/8	f/8 ↓ 11	f/5.6
PLUS-X Pan	f/11	f/8	f/8 ↓ 11	f/5.6
TRI-X Pan	f/22	f/16	f/16 ↓ 22	f/11

FILTERS FOR USE WITH BLACK-AND-WHITE AND COLOR FILMS

Since polarizing screens and neutral density filters do not change the color rendition of a scene, you can use them with both black-and-white and color films.

POLARIZING SCREENS

Polarizing screens do three things that are useful to a photographer. They darken blue skies, they remove or reduce reflections from nonmetallic surfaces such as water and glass, and they penetrate haze.

How Polarizing Screens Work

Polarized Light

To understand how polarizing screens work, you need to know a few things about the nature of light. Light rays travel in straight lines. Light rays also vibrate in all directions perpendicular to their direction of travel. When a light ray hits a nonmetallic surface, the vibration in only one direction, or plane, is reflected completely. (*All* vibrations are reflected by a bare metallic surface.) Depending upon the angle at which you're viewing the light reflected from an object, vibrations in other planes are reduced or eliminated completely. This reflected light —vibrating in only one plane—is called polarized light. The light from a blue sky is polarized because it is reflected off the nonmetallic particles in the atmosphere.

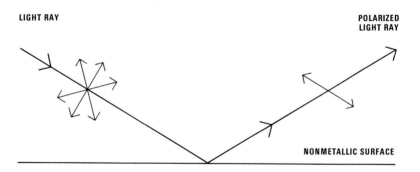

When a light ray from the sun hits a nonmetallic particle in the atmosphere (or any other nonmetallic surface), vibrations of the light ray in only one plane are reflected completely. This reflected light travels at a right angle to the sun and is called polarized light.

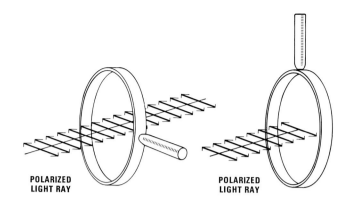

POLARIZED LIGHT RAY

POLARIZED LIGHT RAY

In the drawing on the left, the polarizing screen is transmitting the light vibration of polarized light, and it has no effect on reflections or the sky. In the drawing on the right, the polarizing screen has been rotated 90 degrees. In this position, the polarizing screen absorbs the polarized light so that it removes reflections or darkens the blue sky.

How a Polarizing Screen Affects Polarized Light

A polarizing screen will pass the vibration of a light ray in one plane. Some polarizing screens have handles, and these screens pass the light vibration in a plane parallel to the handle. When the polarizing screen is passing the light vibration of *polarized light,* you'll see no effect on reflections or the sky. Rotate the polarizing screen 90 degrees. In this position, the screen will not transmit the polarized light, so it removes reflections and darkens the blue sky. *Polarizing screens will work only with polarized light because polarized light vibrates in one direction and the polarizing screen can eliminate that vibration.* If you look through a polarizing screen and rotate it until you see its maximum darkening effect, you'll see some light still reflecting from the scene. This light is the nonpolarized light in the scene and the polarized light vibrating in the plane that the screen will transmit. You'll use this light to take the picture.

If you want to get the maximum effect with a polarizing screen, the angle at which you view the reflecting light must equal the angle of the sun (or the original light source) to the reflecting surface. For example, if the sun is shining on water at a 60-degree angle, you'll get the maximum effect with a polarizing screen when you take the picture at a 60-degree angle to the water's surface.

Exposure

A polarizing screen has a filter factor of 2.5 (increase exposure by 1⅓ stops). *This filter factor applies regardless of how much you rotate the polarizing screen.* In addition to this exposure increase for the polarizing screen, you must make any exposure increases required by the nature of the lighting. For example, for the dark-sky effect, the scene must be side-lighted or toplighted, so you'll need to add approximately ½-stop exposure to the 1⅓-stop increase required by the polarizing screen itself.

Allow about an additional ½ stop for subjects that show reflections, because reflections often make subjects look brighter than they are.

KEITH BOAS

Left—taken without a polarizing screen. Right—taken through a polarizing screen.
A polarizing screen, in addition to darkening the blue skies, increases
color saturation in foliage by reducing reflections.

KEITH BOAS

In the comparison picture at the bottom, the polarizing screen
darkened the sky, increased color saturation, and reduced
reflections on the water.

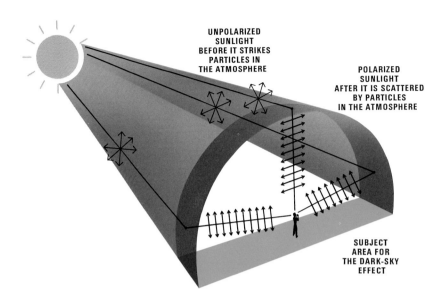

UNPOLARIZED
SUNLIGHT
BEFORE IT STRIKES
PARTICLES IN
THE ATMOSPHERE

POLARIZED
SUNLIGHT
AFTER IT IS SCATTERED
BY PARTICLES
IN THE ATMOSPHERE

SUBJECT
AREA FOR
THE DARK-SKY
EFFECT

You'll get the maximum darkening effect in the sky when you're taking pictures at right angles to the sun and the handle of the polarizing screen (if it has one) is pointing at the sun.

Dark-Sky Effects

The only way you can darken a blue sky in color photography without changing the other colors in the scene is to use a polarizing screen. You'll get the maximum darkening effect when you're taking pictures at right angles to the sun and the handle of the polarizing screen (if it has one) is pointing at the sun. You can obtain various effects from light to dark by rotating the polarizing screen, and you can see the effect you'll get by looking through the screen. After you decide which position of the screen produces the effect you want, be sure to keep the screen in that position when you put it over the camera lens. For example, if the handle was in the 3 o'clock position, make sure it's in the same position when the screen is on the camera. If you have a single-lens reflex camera, you can see the effect of the polarizing screen by looking through the viewfinder while you rotate the screen.

Controlling Reflections

You can improve color saturation with a polarizing screen because it reduces reflections which desaturate the colors. You can also reduce annoying reflections in scenes that include water,

RALPH AMDURSKY

Left—The normal, unpolarized scene on KODACHROME 64 Film (Daylight).

Right—A polarizing screen can eliminate reflections on nonmetallic surfaces and often emphasizes the detail in your pictures.

glass, or other shiny surfaces. Look through the polarizing screen while rotating it to see how you can control the reflections. As we said before, getting the maximum effect with a polarizing screen depends upon your angle to the subject as well as the rotation of the screen. If you can't remove the reflection completely, try changing your angle to the subject. Don't expect to control reflections from bare metal surfaces, because the light reflected from these surfaces is not polarized and the screen will have no effect.

H. ARCHER

When you use neutral density filters to reduce exposure, you can use slow shutter speeds (1/15 sec or slower) to pan with the action and get blurred backgrounds.

NEUTRAL DENSITY FILTERS FOR REDUCING EXPOSURE

Neutral density filters reduce the amount of light passing through your camera lens without changing the rendition of the colors in the scene. You may need to use a neutral density filter when you're taking pictures of a brilliant subject in sunlight with a high-speed film. If you set the fastest shutter speed and the smallest lens opening on your camera and still can't photograph a bright scene without

overexposing it, you can reduce the exposure further by using neutral density filters.

You can also use neutral density filters to reduce the exposure if you want to use large lens openings under bright lighting conditions. With large lens openings, depth of field is very shallow, and you'll get a blurred, out-of-focus background which looks especially pleasing for pictures of people or close-ups of flowers. When you're photographing fast action, you may want to use a slow shutter speed so that you can pan with the action to get a blurred background with the moving subject in sharp focus. If setting the smallest lens opening on your camera still gives too much exposure, you can reduce the exposure with neutral density filters.

Neutral density filters are supplied in various densities, and if necessary you can use two filters together to create the density you want. The table below shows the density values of

Neutral Density Filters

Density	Reduces Exposure by (*f*-stops)
0.10	1/3
0.20	2/3
0.30	1
0.40	1 1/3
0.50	1 2/3
0.60	2
0.70	2 1/3
0.80	2 2/3
0.90	3
1.00	3 1/3

neutral density filters and tells how much each filter reduces exposure. You will probably find the .30, .60, and .90 densities most useful, because they reduce the exposure by 1 stop, 2 stops, and 3 stops, respectively.

FILTERS FOR COLOR PICTURES

In the last chapter we discussed how a polarizing screen can affect your black-and-white and color pictures. Another filter often used with color films is a skylight filter.

Skylight filters, available to fit most cameras, are almost clear and require no exposure compensation.

SKYLIGHT FILTERS

A skylight filter reduces the bluishness of scenes photographed in open shade or on heavily overcast days. It also reduces the bluishness of distant scenes. This reduction of bluishness minimizes the viewer's impression of haze in the scene, but a skylight filter does not actually cut through the dust or vapor to improve the visibility of distant details.

While you might want to keep a skylight filter on your camera all the time to protect the lens from dirt and scratches, the filter will show an effect only with daylight color-slide films. The photofinisher can correct any excessive bluishness in prints made from color negatives. Because a skylight filter absorbs the ultraviolet radiation and only a small amount of blue light, you do not need to increase the exposure when you use this filter.

CONVERSION FILTERS

Color films are balanced for specific light sources. As long as you use a film with its recommended light source, you don't need a filter to get the correct color rendition. When you can't use the recommended light source, you can still get good color rendition by using a conversion filter. Conversion filters change the color quality of a light source to match the quality of the light for which a color film is balanced. For example, you can expose daylight-type films with tungsten light (3200 K) as the light source by using a No. 80A filter. You can use a No. 85B filter to expose tungsten films in daylight, or a No. 85 filter to expose Type A films in daylight. The table on page 29 shows which filter to use with various film and light combinations. The table also gives film speeds that compensate for the light absorbed by the filters.

PETER GALES

KODAK High Speed EKTACHROME
Film (Daylight) exposed to tungsten
illumination (3200 K) without a filter.

KODAK High Speed EKTACHROME
Film (Daylight) exposed to tungsten
illumination (3200 K) through a
No. 80A filter.

KODAK High Speed
EKTACHROME Film
(Tungsten) exposed to
daylight without a filter.

KEITH BOAS

KODAK High Speed
EKTACHROME Film
(Tungsten) exposed to
daylight through a
No. 85B filter.

28

Conversion Filters for KODAK Color Films

KODAK Color Films	Balanced for	Film Speed and Filter		
		Daylight	Photolamp (3400 K)	Tungsten (3200 K)
KODACOLOR II	Daylight, Blue Flash, or Electronic Flash	**80** No filter	**25** No. 80B	**20** No. 80A
KODACHROME 25 (Daylight)		**25** No filter	**8** No. 80B	**6** No. 80A
KODACHROME II Professional (Type A)	Photolamps (3400 K)	**25** No. 85	**40** No filter	**32** No. 82A
KODACHROME 64 and EKTACHROME-X	Daylight, Blue Flash, or Electronic Flash	**64** No filter	**20** No. 80B	**16** No. 80A
High Speed EKTACHROME (Daylight)		**160** No filter	**50** No. 80B	**40** No. 80A
High Speed EKTACHROME (Tungsten)	Tungsten (3200 K)	**80** No. 85B	**100** No. 81A	**125** No filter

Note: The film speeds are printed in **boldface** type.

KODACHROME II
Professional Film (Type A)
exposed to daylight without
a filter.

KODACHROME II
Professional Film (Type A)
exposed to daylight through
a No. 85 filter.

KEITH BOAS

Color pictures taken under fluorescent illumination often have a greenish cast.

KEITH BOAS

By using the filtration recommended in the table below, you can obtain the correct color rendition in scenes illuminated by fluorescent light.

KODAK COLOR COMPENSATING FILTERS

KODAK Color Compensating Filters differ from conversion filters in that they control only the red, blue, or green part of the spectrum and allow the other two colors to pass through. CC (Color Compensating) filters are used mostly in color printing when several different filters are combined. You can also use them in picture-taking with unusual light sources or to create unusual effects.

The first two numbers in the filter designation indicate the density of the filter to the complementary color of light; the final letter indicates the color of the filter. For example, in the designation CC20Y, CC stands for Color Compensating, 20 for a density

of 0.20 to blue light, and Y for yellow.

Pictures taken with daylight-type films under fluorescent illumination often have a greenish cast; pictures made on Type A and tungsten films have a bluish cast. You can correct the color rendition by using CC filters over the camera lens. The table below tells you which filters to use and how much you have to increase the exposure to compensate for the light absorbed by the filters.

CC filters can also help you to compensate for peculiar light absorptions, such as in taking pictures through tinted glass. Use a filter that is the complement of the tint of the glass. For example, with green glass, use a magenta filter.

Filters for Fluorescent Light

Type of Fluorescent Lamp	Type of KODAK Color Film		
	Daylight Type	Tungsten and Type L	Type A
Daylight	40M + 30Y + 1 stop*	No. 85B + 30M + 10Y + 1 stop	No. 85 + 30M + 10Y + 1 stop
White	20C + 30M + 1 stop	40M + 40Y + 1 stop	40M + 30Y + 1 stop
Warm White	40C + 40M + 1⅓ stop	30M + 20Y + 1 stop	30M + 10Y + 1 stop
Warm White Deluxe	60C + 30M + 1⅔ stop	10Y + ⅓ stop	No Filter None
Cool White	30M + ⅔ stop	50M + 60Y + 1⅓ stop	50M + 50Y + 1⅓ stop
Cool White Deluxe	30C + 20M + 1 stop	10M + 30Y + ⅔ stop	10M + 20Y + ⅔ stop

Note: Increase exposure by amount shown in table.
*For KODACHROME 25 and 64 Films, use 40C + 30Y + 1 stop.

KEN BIGGS

Place a warm-colored filter, such as a No. 25 red filter, in front of the camera lens to add dramatic color to a sunset.

USING FILTERS FOR CREATIVE EFFECTS

You can use filters to create unusual effects by introducing additional color into your pictures. You can also enhance the mood of a picture by using filters. For example, it's easy to add color to a sunset by photographing it through a deep yellow or red filter. The filter may make the difference between an ordinary shot and a prize-winning picture. To simulate moonlight in a sunlit scene, use a blue filter and underexpose the picture by about two stops. This technique works well with scenes including water or snow.

You can also use filters to add color to your slides after they have been processed. Just mount a piece of gelatin filter right in with your slide. This technique is a good one to apply to your slightly overexposed slides, because the filter will add both color and density to the slide.

The picture on the top shows the scene as it actually appeared in sunlight.
In the comparison picture on the bottom, the photographer simulated moonlight by
using a deep blue filter and deliberately underexposing the scene.

A No. 11 yellow-green filter gave this picture impact by
increasing color saturation in both the greens of the background
and the spider's yellow markings.

A No. 25 red filter with
KODACOLOR II Film.

A piece of a No. 21 orange gelatin filter bound with this slide made on
KODAK EKTACHROME-X Film produced the dramatic effect and
salvaged a nearly colorless picture.

MULTIPLE EXPOSURES

To make an intriguing picture that will keep your friends wondering how you did it, put your camera on a tripod and make three exposures on the same frame of film. Make the first exposure through a No. 25 red filter, the second exposure through a No. 61 deep green filter, and the third exposure through a No. 38A blue filter. Use a lens hood to avoid lens flare during the three exposures.

To determine your exposure, take a meter reading of the scene; then increase the exposure that the meter indicates by one stop for *each of your three exposures*. For example, the exposure for a sunlit scene with KODACOLOR II Film should be 1/125 second at $f/11$. That means you would use 1/125 second at $f/8$ for the exposure through each of the three filters. You don't need to consider the filter factor when you try this technique. If you select a subject that has some movement, such as a seascape or a landscape on a windy day, you'll get a rainbow of color in the highlight areas of your picture.

You can also photograph action with this multiple-filter technique. Tape the three filters together to make one long strip. At each end of the strip, tape a piece of black cardboard. With your camera set on B or T, open the shutter and quickly pass the entire strip in front of the lens, beginning and ending with the black cardboard pieces. The cardboard at the beginning of the strip blocks any light from entering the camera until you are ready to pass the filters in front of the lens. The cardboard at the end of the strip blocks the lens after you have made the exposure. Exposure time depends on how fast the three filters pass in front of the lens. *The Seventh*

ROBERT HARRIS

This picture is a triple exposure, with each exposure made through a filter of a different color. The red, green, and blue filters put the colors in the moving white steam.

Here's How, KODAK Publication No. AE-90, gives all the details on assembling and using a three-filter strip.

For best results with this technique, use a color-negative film such as KODACOLOR II Film. Negative films are easy to work with when you're trying multiple exposures because they have more exposure latitude. You can always ask your photo dealer to have slides made from your processed negatives if you would rather have slides than prints.

This interesting double exposure was made through a light magenta filter
and a cyan filter. Each exposure was reduced from normal by about two *f*-stops
to allow the tree branches to register against the light sky.

ROBERT HARRIS

The red, green, and blue filters used to make this triple exposure add subtle color
to the movements of the runner. The three separate exposures were made
in a fraction of a second by passing the three filters in front of the lens while
the shutter remained open. To keep the runner centered during the exposure,
the photographer followed the action by panning the camera.

Use a color-negative film such as
KODACOLOR II Film to make triple exposures
with filters. The latitude of the film gives
you more exposure flexibility.

NEIL MONTANUS

SPLIT FILTERING

Gelatin filter squares give you the flexibility of changing or adding color in only a part of a scene. They also let you vary two or more colors at the same time during a single exposure. To change or darken the color of the sky in your picture, for example, place a gelatin filter over the top part of the lens, filtering only the sky. Base your exposure on the ground (nonfiltered) area of the scene. The resulting sky area in the picture should closely match the ground area in image density, since the filter will have reduced the brightness of the sky.

You can use two or more filters in this same way by butting them together along their edges. This will give you the opportunity to add or change color selectively and thereby create an unusual multiple-color rendition of your subject. Assemble this split (or multiple) filter by taping strips of gelatin filters into a KODAK Gelatin Filter Frame. Either hold this combination of filters extremely close to the lens or slip it into a filter holder mounted on the front of the lens. The closer to the lens you place the filters, the softer will be the blend between one filter edge and another in the picture. When using more than one filter, choose filters which have the same or similar filter factors so that you can maintain a reasonably balanced exposure throughout the entire picture area.

This picture was made without a filter on KODAK EKTACHROME-X Film.

To make a split-field multicolored filter, cut strips of gelatin filter to fit into a filter frame. Butt the edges together and tape the filters in place. To see what results you can expect from a split-field blue/red filter, turn to page 40.

A No. 25 red gelatin filter was placed over the top half of the camera lens to filter only the sky. No exposure compensation was made. Note that the added density has the additional effect of reducing the flare from the sun.

The unfiltered picture at the top shows the correct color of the water. The center picture was made with a No. 25 red gelatin filter covering the top half of the lens and a No. 47 blue gelatin filter covering the bottom half. The picture at the bottom shows the effect of reversing the positions of the same two filters.

KEITH BOAS

You can make your own filters for creative effects with Fun Film™ and some loops of wire. If you want a clear opening in the filter, use a razor-edged knife to cut out the center after the film is dry. The completed filter can be held or attached in front of the lens during exposure.

MAKING YOUR OWN FILTERS

If you are interested in adding some bright color to all or part of a picture, you might like to consider a material such as Fun Film™, available through hobby stores. You can make the support for your filter by forming a wire loop a little larger in diameter than the camera lens. Then dip the loop into a container of Fun Film and slowly remove it so that a thin film of the colored material remains across the wire. Once it's dry, about a minute or two later, you can cut an opening in the filter with a razor-edged knife if you want only partial filtration.

Attach the filter to the front of your camera lens with tape, wire, or a rubber band, and you are ready to take a picture. If you are using a tripod, you may prefer to hand-hold the filter in front of the lens to gain more flexibility in positioning it for the effect you want.

These homemade filters will produce colorful and unusual results; however, they may also cause unwanted distortions. Plan on using them for special effects only and not as substitutes for filters of the conventional type.

NEIL MONTANUS

To create this evening effect, a black-and-white enlargement was copied on High Speed EKTACHROME Film through a deep blue filter.

A filter made with poppy-red Fun Film™ was used in combination with a No. 15 deep-yellow filter.

COLOR SLIDES FROM BLACK-AND-WHITE PRINTS

For a color interpretation of a black-and-white print, try copying the print through a filter. You can produce slides of any color you desire, in any intensity, simply by selecting the appropriate color filter. Filters with heavy color saturation which are designed for use in black-and-white photography will generally give you the most dramatic results. A No. 47 blue filter, for example, can heighten the mood in night and water scenes, while a No. 25 red filter might enhance a sunset or low-key portrait.

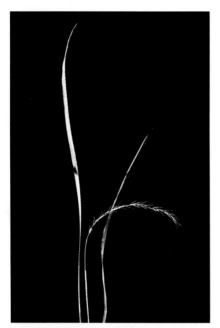

The original black-and-white print.

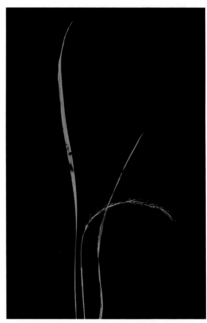

No. 58 green filter.

No. 15 deep-yellow filter.

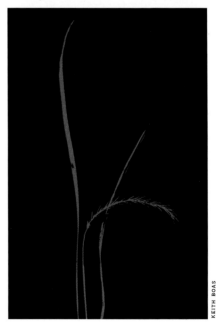

No. 25 red filter.

SPECIAL-EFFECTS ATTACHMENTS

Manufacturers of photo equipment go to considerable lengths to design lenses capable of producing sharp, distortion-free images. Therefore, it may surprise you when we suggest that you risk hindering this image quality by changing the light path with a lens attachment. However, while attachments may reduce sharpness to some extent, the wealth of effects they can create usually more than makes up for any image-quality loss. Lens attachments, like filters, can expand your picture-taking horizons. With a diffraction grating, for example, you can add striking color to a nearly colorless scene. A multiple-image attachment can give you an interesting pattern picture, and a cross screen will put star-shape flares in highlight areas of still lifes, water, and night scenes.

Lens attachments, used alone or in combination with filters, can serve as effective tools to help you create your own subjective interpretation of a scene. Lens attachments for creating unusual effects are supplied by several companies, including those listed on page 6.

DON MAGGIO

Soft-focus attachments are relatively clear and transmit nearly all of the light, so exposure adjustments aren't necessary.

With a soft-focus attachment over
your camera lens, you can produce
diffused, subdued images.

DON MAGGIO

You can make your own soft-focus attachment
by smearing petroleum jelly on a piece of
transparent glass. Here, the center of the glass
was kept clear, allowing the bride's head
and shoulders to remain sharp.

NORM KERR

Soft-focus attachments generally work best in making evenly lighted portraits of women and children and in photographing passive subjects such as flowers.

Commercially made soft-focus attachments offer a range of picture-taking effects from overall mistiness to only partial diffusion.

A soft-focus attachment and a light magenta filter were combined to create this picture.

The background in the slide on the right was subdued by taking the picture through a small (half-dollar-size) opening in a sheet of matte acetate. Both pictures were taken on KODACHROME 64 Film (Daylight).

SOFT-FOCUS EFFECTS

You can place a variety of materials in front of your camera lens to create a dreamlike or subdued effect. You might want to soften the sharpness only slightly while making a portrait of a young girl. In a close-up of a wild flower, you might prefer to create a colorful blur by heavily diffusing the picture area surrounding the blossom. Several commercially available attachments give you a choice of how much of your picture will be diffused and to what extent. Regardless of the attachment you select, the glass is relatively clear and transmits nearly all the light, so you won't have to make exposure adjustments.

You might like to try constructing your own diffusing attachment. There are several ways to go about it, and each method produces a slightly different result. Petroleum jelly smeared on a clean, transparent piece of glass

or acetate sheeting makes a very effective diffuser. Start with an almost clear glass filter such as a No. 1A skylight filter, and apply a thin coat of petroleum jelly to the front surface. Leave the center of the glass untouched if you want part of your picture to remain sharp.

Instead of glass, you can use a sheet of clear acetate. Cut a 75 mm (3-inch) square from one corner to fit into a 75 mm (3-inch) KODAK Gelatin Filter Holder. Place the acetate square in a KODAK Gelatin Filter Frame to keep it rigid. Then apply a thin coat of the petroleum jelly to the sheet. You can make straight lines in the coating by lightly dragging a stiff brush through it. These straight lines will refract the light passing through the coated acetate in a definite pattern and add interest to the diffused portion of the image. Whether you use glass or acetate, you can increase the amount of diffusion by adding a heavier layer of petroleum jelly.

For heavy diffusion in all but the center of your picture, use a sheet of matte acetate. Cut a hole the size of a quarter in the center of the sheet. Then place the sheet in front of your lens, using the KODAK Gelatin Filter Holder and Filter Frame.

This technique works particularly well with telephoto lenses. Normal and wide-angle lenses tend to show the hole in the acetate as a noticeable edge. You can soften the edge somewhat by placing the acetate sheet as close to the lens as possible and using a large lens opening. But as you increase the lens opening, you must correspondingly reset your shutter speed to a faster setting to maintain the same exposure. This may be a problem in bright-sun conditions with medium- and high-speed films. KODACOLOR II, KODACHROME 64, and KODAK EKTACHROME-X Films used in bright sun would require a basic exposure of $f/4$ at $1/1000$ second. To open the lens to $f/2.8$ without increasing exposure, you can use a .3 neutral density filter. There is enough room in the Gelatin Filter Frame for both the matte acetate and the neutral density filter.

To reduce exposure even further without changing the f-number or shutter speed, use more than one neutral density filter or one with a greater absorption capability. See the chart on page 26 for help in selecting the right filter density.

KEITH BOAS

To produce a low-key vignette such as that at the bottom, cover your camera lens with a piece of opaque construction paper or cardboard that has an opening cut in the middle. If your camera has a behind-the-lens metering system, determine your exposure *before* covering the lens with the opaque vignetter.

VIGNETTING

The matte-acetate technique described above will produce a high-key vignetted picture. To achieve a low-key vignette in which the picture shades off into black at the edges, use a piece of opaque construction paper or cardboard. With a razor-edge knife, cut a hole in the middle, fasten the remaining opaque material to the front of the lens, and shoot through the opening. The surface which faces the lens should be dull black to avoid any chance of reflecting ambient light into the lens. You will have to do some experimenting to determine the size of the opening that will produce the best vignette with your particular lens opening and focal length.

This opaque vignette attachment highlights your center of interest simply by eliminating the surrounding scene. It works especially well for close-ups of subjects posed against dark or subdued backgrounds. To simulate an old-fashioned photograph, combine a soft-focus attachment with the opaque vignetter. To imitate the warm, pastel photographic style of the 1930s, add to this "sandwich" a CC30Y filter.

CROSS SCREENS

Though pictures of night scenes and subjects showing specular highlights are usually dramatic in themselves, there are ways to make them even more so. Point sources of light, when photographed through some form of screened material, can be recorded

as appealing starlike patterns. The effect can often give a scene a jewel-like quality. The brighter and smaller the light source or specular highlight in the scene, the greater the light-scattering effect will be.

Commercially available cross-screen lens attachments, supplied in various grids, produce right-angle, four-pointed stars around small light sources and specular highlights. Two cross screens, when rotated at an angle to one another, make eight-pointed stars. If you are using a single-lens reflex camera, look through your viewfinder and rotate the outer screen until you see the effect you want. To compensate for the light absorbed by the screen, allow about ½ stop more exposure for each layer of screen you use.

If you want to try cross-screen photography right away but don't have a commercially designed attachment, you might like to try making your own.

The grid arrangement of a cross-screen attachment can scatter the direct light from the sun into an interesting four-pointed, right-angle pattern.

Use a piece of window screen to make your own cross-screen attachment. For easy handling, trim the screen and slip it into a KODAK Gelatin Filter Frame.

NORM KERR

51

The cross-star effect in this night scene was produced by placing a
piece of window screen in front of the camera lens.

Take a piece of window-screen material and place it over your lens. If you don't have any screening around your workshop, just visit your local hardware store. You'll need a piece of screen large enough to cover the front of the lens—a 3-inch-square piece if you want to slip it into a 75 mm (3-inch) KODAK Gelatin Filter Holder. You can also attach the screen to your camera by cutting it to fit an adapter ring and then placing the adapter ring on the lens.

MULTIPLE-IMAGE LENSES

Multiple-image lenses offer an exciting dimension in creative interpretation with both still and movie cameras. These lenses are specially designed pieces of glass that fit on the front of your camera lens. Since they transmit nearly 100 percent of the light, there is no need for exposure compensation. Multiple-image lenses are multi-surfaced in such a way that they can divide a single subject into several identical images. Depending on which multiple-image lens you choose, you have the capability of recording these repeating images in concentric, radial, or linear patterns.

With a single-lens reflex camera, you can see the effect the lens produces right in your viewfinder. Simply rotate the lens accessory until your multiple subjects appear in a pleasing composition. A subject with a simple background takes on a dreamlike quality, while a busy scene can split into a wild, nervous collage.

Multiple-image lenses are easy to use. After choosing your subject, select a pleasing composition by rotating the glass, and then make your exposure.

A junkyard takes on a frantic aspect when photographed with a linear-patterned multiple-image lens.

Subjects with simple backgrounds usually lend themselves best to photography with a multiple-image lens.

Enhance the repeating-pattern effect by adding a piece of gelatin filter to each surface of the multiple-image lens. Hold each filter piece in place with dabs of transparent tape along the edges that touch the rim of the lens attachment.

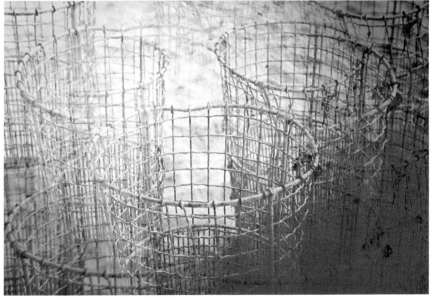

TRANSMISSION DIFFRACTION GRATINGS

A transmission diffraction grating is a piece of glass or plastic which has thousands of precisely spaced ridges on its surface. These ridges act as prisms; they reveal the color spectrum of white light. When you look at light through a transmission diffraction grating, you can see the colors of the spectrum. The amount of color you see is determined by the spacing of the ridges on the grating and the angle at which you're viewing them.

You can use a transmission diffraction grating over your lens to create unusual effects and to add color to your pictures. There is no exposure change with a diffraction grating, and you just hold it in front of the camera lens while you take a picture. If you have a single-lens reflex camera, you can see the effect of the diffraction grating by looking through the viewfinder while you rotate the grating. With other cameras, first look through the grating while you rotate it. Then when you see the effect you want, be sure to keep the grating in that position as you put it over the camera lens.

Transmission diffraction gratings, which are made of acetate plastic, come in sheets 8½ x 11 inches and in rolls 8½ inches wide by 6 feet long. The grating is inexpensive, and you can cut one sheet into six 3-inch diffraction gratings.

To protect your diffraction grating and make it easier to handle, cut a 3-inch-square piece of grating out of one corner of the sheet. Slip this square into a 75 mm (3-inch) KODAK Gelatin Filter Frame. The filter frame will hold the diffraction grating in a flat plane and allow you to use the grating without getting fingerprints on it. When the diffraction grating in the filter frame becomes scratched and

A transmission diffraction grating adds color to your pictures by revealing the colors contained in white light.

dirty from use, replace it with another piece of grating from your sheet. Store the sheet of diffraction grating between the two pieces of cardboard in the original package.

You can order transmission diffraction gratings from scientific or hobby-supply companies, such as Edmund Scientific Company, 150 Edscorp Building, Barrington, New Jersey 08007, and Spiratone, Inc., 135-06 Northern Blvd., Flushing, New York 11354.

57

DON MAGGIO

The exaggerated image distortion produced by a fisheye lens attachment gives it wide application for dramatic pictures in sports, nature, and architectural photography.

FISHEYE EFFECTS

A fisheye lens, so named because of its ability to cover an extremely wide angle of view similar to that which a fish sees, is an ideal accessory for creating pictures with unusual impact. A fisheye lens accessory can be easily mounted on the front of most 35 mm and 2¼ x 2¼-inch camera lenses. With most lenses, you can expect a considerable increase in the angle of view. By attaching a fisheye accessory to the front of the lens, you can achieve an angle of about three to four times as great, depending on which manufacturer's accessory you use. With a normal or wide-angle lens, it's possi-ble to obtain an angle approaching 180 degrees—so wide, in fact, that you must take care not to include your feet in the picture!

Besides its tremendous wide-angle capability, a fisheye lens accessory also has a remarkable depth-of-field range. If you use it with a normal lens focused at infinity, everything from about three feet to infinity will be acceptably sharp at a wide-open lens aperture. Set your camera lens at its minimum focusing distance, and objects as close as one-half inch from the camera will be in sharp focus, depending on the lens opening you use.

KEITH BOAS

To produce this nearly 180-degree view, the photographer added a fisheye lens attachment to a normal 50 mm lens on a 35 mm camera. The prime (50 mm) lens was set at its widest aperture and the f-number was controlled by the aperture scale on the fisheye lens attachment (1/250 sec at f/8 on KODACOLOR II Film).

59

In the picture on the opposite page, the wild flowers were only a few inches away from the camera. To record both nearby flowers and distant mountains in proper focus, the photographer used a split-field attachment. The camera was focused at infinity.

SPLIT-FIELD EFFECTS

As you view a scene, your mind allows you to take in all the elements, both near and far, in proper focus. Most camera lenses, though, with perhaps the exception of the fisheye lens, don't have this infinite depth-of-field ability, even when stopped down to their smallest lens openings. But a split-field lens attachment can record amazing near/far sharpness in a single exposure at any lens opening.

Basically, a split-field attachment incorporates half a close-up lens. The half of the attachment which contains the lens serves as a close-up attachment for a nearby subject. The other half of the attachment is empty, allowing the camera lens to focus normally through its full distance range. Once the attachment is mounted on the camera, you can rotate it to position the close-up half over the half of the camera lens that will be recording the nearby subject. For best results, use the attachment on a single-lens reflex camera so that you can see the effect and the degree of foreground sharpness before you take the picture.

When you take pictures with close-up attachments, the range of sharp focus is very shallow, making it necessary to focus carefully.

CLOSE-UP AND TELEPHOTO ATTACHMENTS

You can take pictures from as close as 2½ to 3 feet with most adjustable cameras, but for really dramatic close-up pictures you need to get even closer to your subject. You can take extreme close-ups by using close-up lenses or, if your camera is designed to accept them, extension tubes or bellows. Any of these aids will allow you to move in close enough to fill your picture area with small subjects.

CLOSE-UP LENSES

One advantage of using close-up lenses rather than lens-extension devices is that you use normal exposures. (Extension devices often require an increase in exposure, which usually means more figuring.) Close-up lenses are also inexpensive and are generally all you need in addition to the camera and film. (With some cameras, an adapter ring and retaining ring may be needed to hold the close-up lens in place.)

Close-up lenses come in different sizes—designated by a series number or by the diameter in millimeters—to fit different camera lenses. Consult your camera manual to learn what size of close-up lens and adapter ring (if any) your camera needs. Your photo dealer can also measure your camera lens to determine what series of lens attachments it accepts. Eastman Kodak Company does not produce close-up lenses, but they are supplied by other companies, including these:

Ponder & Best, Inc., 1630 Stewart St., Santa Monica, California 90406

P.R.O., Inc., 159 W. 33rd St., New York, New York 10001

Spiratone, Inc., 130 W. 31st St., New York, New York 10001

Tiffen Optical Co., 71 Jane St., Roslyn Heights, New York 11577

Uniphot, Inc., 61-10 34th Ave., Woodside, New York 11377

Close-up lenses are available in different strengths or powers, such as +1, +2, and +3. The higher the number, the stronger the lens and the closer you can get to your subject. You can use two close-up lenses together to work at even closer distances. For example, a +2 lens and a +3 lens equal a +5 lens. When you use two close-up lenses together, the stronger lens should be closer to the camera. More than two lenses used together may result in poor image quality and may cut off the corners of the image.

In close-up picture-taking, depth of field is very shallow. Since the range of sharp focus for a close-up lens may be only a fraction of an inch, the distance between the lens and the subject to be photographed is critical.

Close-Up Data for KODAK INSTAMATIC® Cameras

KODAK INSTAMATIC Cameras	Close-Up Lens +1		Close-Up Lens +2		Close-Up Lens +3		Close-Up Lens +5 (+2 + +3)	
	SUBJECT DISTANCE	FIELD SIZE (Square)	SUBJECT DISTANCE	FIELD SIZE (Square)	SUBJECT DISTANCE	FIELD SIZE (Square)	SUBJECT DISTANCE	FIELD SIZE (Square)
100, 104, 124, 134, 150, 154, 174, X-15, and X-25	30	18 1/2	17	10	12	7 1/2	7 1/2	4 3/4
300, 304, 400, and 404 or 314, 414, X-35, and X-45 focused for beyond 6 feet	30	19 1/2	17	11	12	7 1/2	7 1/2	4 3/4
314, 414, X-35, and X-45 focused for 2 to 6 feet	21 1/2	13 3/4	14	9	10 1/4	6 1/2	6 3/4	4 1/4
S-10 and S-20	30	23	17	13	12	9	7 1/2	5 1/2

63

Close-Up Data for
KODAK INSTAMATIC 700, 704, 714, 800, 804, 814, and X-90 Cameras

FOCUS SETTING (feet)	Close-Up Lens +1		Close-Up Lens +2		Close-Up Lens +3	
	SUBJECT DISTANCE	FIELD SIZE (Square)	SUBJECT DISTANCE	FIELD SIZE (Square)	SUBJECT DISTANCE	FIELD SIZE (Square)
Inf	39	27 1/2	19 1/2	13 1/2	13 1/8	9 1/4
50	37	26	19 1/8	13	12 3/4	9
25	34 3/4	24 1/4	18 1/2	12 3/4	12 3/8	8 3/4
10	29 5/8	21	16 7/8	11 3/4	11 3/4	8 1/4
6	25 1/2	18	15 1/2	10 1/2	11 1/8	7 3/4
4	21 5/8	15	13 3/4	9 1/2	10 1/8	7
3	18 7/8	13 1/4	12 3/8	8 1/2	9 3/4	6 1/2

Close-Up Data for 35 mm Cameras

Close-up Lens and Focus Setting (in feet)		Lens-to-Subject Distance (in inches)	Approximate Field Size (in inches)	
			44—46 mm Lens on a 35 mm Camera	50 mm Lens on a 35 mm Camera
+1	Inf	39	20 x 29 3/4	18 x 26 3/4
	15	32 1/4	16 1/2 x 24 1/2	14 3/4 x 22
	6	25 1/2	13 x 19 1/4	11 3/4 x 17 1/4
	3 1/2	20 3/8	10 3/8 x 15 1/4	9 3/8 x 13 3/4
+2	Inf	19 1/2	10 1/8 x 15	9 x 13 1/2
	15	17 3/4	9 1/8 x 13 1/2	8 1/8 x 12
	6	15 1/2	7 7/8 x 11 3/4	7 1/8 x 10 1/2
	3 1/2	13 3/8	6 7/8 x 10 1/8	6 1/8 x 9 1/8
+3	Inf	13 1/8	6 3/4 x 9 7/8	6 x 8 7/8
	15	12 1/4	6 1/4 x 9 1/4	5 5/8 x 8 3/8
	6	11 1/8	5 5/8 x 8 3/8	5 1/8 x 7 1/2
	3 1/2	10	5 1/8 x 7 1/2	4 5/8 x 6 3/4
+3 plus +1	Inf	9 7/8	5 x 7 3/8	4 1/2 x 6 5/8
	15	9 3/8	4 3/4 x 7	4 1/4 x 6 3/8
	6	8 5/8	4 3/8 x 6 3/8	4 x 5 7/8
	3 1/2	8	4 1/8 x 6	3 5/8 x 5 3/8
+3 plus +2	Inf	7 7/8	4 x 5 7/8	3 5/8 x 5 3/8
	15	7 1/2	3 7/8 x 5 3/4	3 1/2 x 5 1/8
	6	7 1/8	3 5/8 x 5 3/8	3 1/4 x 4 7/8
	3 1/2	6 5/8	3 3/8 x 5	3 x 4 1/2
+3 plus +3	Inf	6 5/8	3 3/8 x 5	3 x 4 1/2
	15	6 3/8	3 1/4 x 4 3/4	2 7/8 x 4 1/4
	6	6	3 1/8 x 4 1/2	2 3/4 x 4 1/8
	3 1/2	5 5/8	2 7/8 x 4 1/4	2 5/8 x 3 7/8

NORM KERR

When you look through the view-finder of a single-lens reflex camera, you can see whether the picture will be sharp and properly framed because you're looking directly through the lens that takes the picture. When you use close-up lenses on a nonreflex camera, you can't check the focus by looking through the viewfinder, so *it's important to measure the distance from the close-up lens to the subject.*

After you have the close-up lens mounted on your camera, see the tables on pages 63 and 64. They give the correct distances from the close-up lens to the subject for various camera and lens combinations. They also tell how much area (called field size) will be included in your pictures.

In these three charts, all lens-to-subject distances and field sizes are in inches. Measure the lens-to-subject distance from the front of the close-up lens.

EXTENSION TUBES AND BELLOWS

If your camera will accept extension tubes or bellows, you can make close-up pictures without accessory lenses. Extension tubes and bellows are usually used on single-lens reflex cameras, because with these cameras you can see exactly what will be in the picture and check the focus by looking through the viewfinder. However, when you use bellows or tubes, you may need to increase the exposure to compensate for the light loss that results from the lens extension. To determine what exposure compensation is necessary, see the instructions packaged with your equipment, or use the Lens-Extension Exposure Dial in the *KODAK Master Photoguide* (AR-21) or the Close-Up Exposure Dial in the *KODAK Professional Photoguide* (R-28). These guides are available from photo dealers.

To make this extreme close-up, an extension tube was inserted between the lens and the camera body. The increased lens-to-film distance allowed the coin—only 3½ inches away from the front of the lens—to be in sharp focus.

Three extension tubes were linked to produce this close-up slide. The lighting was provided by electronic flash.

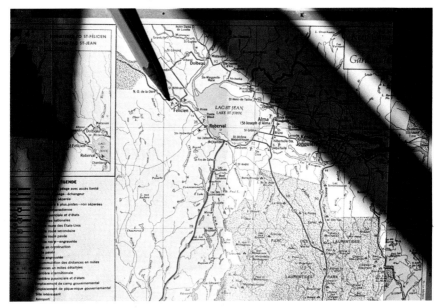

In the picture at the top, the pencil points to the map section to be copied.
The resulting close-up (at the bottom) was made with a bellows attachment between
the lens and the camera body. An exposure compensation of nearly 4 stops
was needed for this 2.4X magnification. Both pictures were taken
on KODACHROME 64 Film (Daylight).

PICTURE-TAKING THROUGH TELESCOPES

An excellent camera for taking pictures through a telescope is the single-lens reflex camera. When you look through the viewfinder of the camera, you are looking through the lens system. This enables you to position the image and focus your telescope/camera system conveniently and accurately. Optical instruments that you can use for obtaining dramatic telescopic effects with your camera include binoculars and spotting scopes as well as astronomical telescopes with eyepieces.

To take pictures with your camera and a telescope, you'll need a simple mounting device to attach the two units. The mounting device should provide both precise alignment of your camera lens with your telescope eyepiece and a rigid, vibration-free support for your camera. Although the mount should furnish a lighttight guard between the two units, this guard is not absolutely necessary. A black, lint-free cloth will do. You can purchase mounting devices for about $15 to $20 from optical-supply firms such as Optica b/c Company, 4100 MacArthur Boulevard, Oakland, California 94619, and Edmund Scientific Company.

Once you have securely mounted your camera and telescope, open the camera lens to its maximum aperture and set it for infinity. Then adjust the focus with your telescope. When the image looks sharp on the ground glass of your viewfinder, it will be sharp on your film.

If you can remove the lens from your camera, you can use an alternate method for picture-taking through a telescope. After removing the lens, align the camera body directly behind the telescope eyepiece. Adjust the camera-to-eyepiece distance so that the image is sharp on the film plane. Although the image will be slightly smaller than if the camera lens had been used, it will be sharper and brighter because there are fewer optical surfaces in the light path.

There are two major classes of telescopes: refracting and reflecting. The refracting telescope forms an image of an object by transmitting the light rays through a lens system similar to that of a camera or binocular. The reflecting telescope collects the light rays with an accurately curved mirror which forms the image. With both telescopes, the primary image is magnified by an eyepiece. Reflecting telescopes are less expensive and are generally better at focusing different colors in the same plane. This feature is important in obtaining sharp photographic images.

Astronomers use the term objective lens, or objective when they refer to the main or primary lens of a telescope, which collects the light from the subject. The objective may be either the objective (front) lens of a refracting telescope or the mirror of a reflecting telescope. The f-number of your telescope/camera system is determined by your telescope. Knowing the size and/or focal length of the objective will help you determine what this f-number is.

You can use one of the formulas on page 70 to find the effective f-number. Use the formula that includes telescope power if you don't know the focal length of your telescope objective or eyepiece but you do know the power of your telescope.

KODACHROME 64 Film (Daylight) was used to record the moon through a 6-inch reflector telescope with a 25 mm eyepiece.

This 6-inch reflector telescope, obtained from Edmund Scientific Company, was used to make the moon picture on page 69.

Using a camera mount, align your camera directly behind the telescope eyepiece. In this setup, the camera lens has been removed.

$$f\text{-number} = \frac{F \times F_c}{D \times F_e}$$

or

$$\frac{\dfrac{\text{Telescope}}{\text{power}} \times F_c}{D}$$

F = focal length of the telescope objective
F_c = focal length of the camera lens
F_e = focal length of the eyepiece
D = diameter of the telescope objective
Note: Use the same units for all dimensions.

Once you've found the f-number, determine the proper shutter speed that would normally be required at that f-number with your particular film and lighting conditions. For example, a full moon is a sunlit subject and would generally require about the same exposure as a sunlit scene here on earth. So if you find your effective f-number to be $f/16$ and are using KODACHROME 64 Film, your exposure would be $f/16$ at $1/60$ second, which is the average sunlight exposure for a film with a speed of ASA 64. However, this exposure would tend to reproduce the moon as a medium gray, which may appear somewhat darker than you would like it to be. Using the next slower shutter speed ($1/30$ second) will give you a moon with better brightness.

A full moon occurs only once every 28 days, and it's a long wait until the next one if you didn't get the picture you wanted the first time. To be more certain of properly exposed pictures, it's a good idea to bracket your exposures. Take a picture at the final calculated exposure; then take another picture at one shutter speed faster, a third picture at one speed slower, and a fourth at two speeds slower.

If you would like to learn more about the hobby of astrophotography, write to Eastman Kodak Company, Photo Information, Dept. 841, Rochester, New York 14650. Ask for a free copy of *Astrophotography with Your Camera,* Publication No. AC-20. Other helpful references are *Photography with Your Telescope,* available from Edmund Scientific Company, and *Star Gazing with Telescope and Camera,* by George T. Keene (Amphoto).

The picture on the left was made with a 200 mm lens. In the example on the right, a 2X teleconverter was added between the 200 mm lens and the camera body to obtain this 400 mm telephoto result. The camera (on a tripod) was in the same location for both pictures. The film was KODAK High Speed EKTACHROME Film (Daylight).

TELECONVERTERS

If you have a camera with interchangeable-lens capability, you might like to consider purchasing an inexpensive telephoto converter (generally called a teleconverter or tele-extender) to change your normal or telephoto camera lens into a lens of higher power. A teleconverter is a supplementary optical accessory which you attach between the camera body and the camera lens. Once in place, it will increase the focal length of the lens—the amount of increase depending on the magnifying power of the teleconverter.

Teleconverters are available in 1½X, 2X, 3X, and zoom magnifications. A 2X converter, for example, will double the focal length and magnification of a lens, while a 3X converter will triple them. Let's say that you have a 200 mm lens for your camera. A 2X converter, when attached between the lens and the camera body, will give you the equivalent of a 400 mm lens. Use a 3X teleconverter with a 200 mm lens to produce a 600 mm lens.

One possible disadvantage in using a teleconverter is a slight loss of image sharpness, particularly at the edges of the picture. Teleconverters also reduce the amount of light which reaches the film. A 2X teleconverter, for example, requires 2 additional stops in exposure compensation. A 2X converter, when used with a 50 mm $f/2.8$ lens, converts it to a 100 mm $f/5.6$ lens. While the results are not quite as sharp as those obtained with most 100 mm prime lenses, the softness produced is often desirable in portraiture. You can improve image sharpness somewhat by stopping down the lens aperture 2 or 3 f-numbers from its maximum, wide-open setting.

Kodak does not manufacture teleconverters, but several companies do offer them in assorted mounts to fit a variety of camera bodies. Check with your local photo shop to see which ones fit your camera.

NORM KERR

CARE AND HANDLING OF FILTERS AND LENS ATTACHMENTS

GELATIN FILTERS

Gelatin filters are easily scratched and damaged, so handle them by the edges only. Remove dust particles by brushing *gently* with a clean, dry camel's-hair brush or by gently blowing clean, dry air across the surfaces. To cut a gelatin filter, place it between two sheets of clean paper for protection while you cut with a pair of sharp scissors. Store these filters in a dust-free container in a cool, dry place.

STABILITY OF FILTERS

Filter dyes may change color in time, particularly when exposed to daylight for long periods of time. Extreme temperatures and high humidity may accelerate a change in color. You can prolong the life of your filters by storing them in a dark, cool, dry place.

GLASS FILTERS AND LENS ATTACHMENTS

Glass filters and lens attachments require the same care and handling as your camera lens. You can clean them with a soft, lintless cloth slightly moistened with KODAK Lens Cleaner. Don't get any moisture on the cemented edges of a filter laminated between glass squares. You can polish glass filters and lens attachments with KODAK Lens Cleaning Paper.

Keep your lens accessories in their original container for protection when you're not using them. Handle them only by the edges to avoid fingerprints, which degrade picture quality.